Faith...
and Star Battles

Thomas Myers

... *Erkanka na Adonai* is Hebrew for *I love you, Lord* - Psalm 18:1

Copyright © 2021 by Thomas Myers

All rights reserved. No part of this publication may be reproduced or transmitted in any form or by any electronic or mechanical means including photo copying, recording, or any information storage and retrieval system now known or to be invented, without permission in writing from the publisher or the author.

All Scripture quotations, unless otherwise indicated, are from The King James Version. The KJV is public domain in the United States.

Publisher's Cataloging-in-Publication data
Name: Myers, Thomas
Faith... And Star Battles
Identifiers: ISBN 978-1-952369-57-5
 LCCN: 2021904041
Subjects: 1. Biography & Autobiography/General
2. Religion/Christian Living/Personal Memoirs

Cover Designer: Krystine Kercher

Cover Image: Adobe Stock 2018

Author Photo: Agape Imaging 2008

Published by EA Books Publishing a division of

Living Parables of Central Florida, Inc. a 501c3

EABooksPublishing.com

Table of Contents

Prologue v

Who Am I? 1

What it Means to be Christian 8

Sexual Purity 15

On Relations 19

Psychology 24

The Bible 27

Scientific Advancements 30

Fate 33

The Church 35

Space-Time Continuum 38

Origin of the Earth 42

Prayer 45

Paradise 48

Review 51

References 53

Endnotes 58

About the Author 61

ACKNOWLEDGMENTS

This manuscript would not be possible without you all:
The Holy Trinity (for obvious reasons).
Joseph and Mary, for raising the Son of God.
My family, for their unwavering support.
St Cecilia Parish and School Staff, for giving me the chance to worship.
Central Crossing High School Staff, for a wonderful four years.
The midshipmen of Task Group Buckeye.
All my language teachers, for inspiring my skills.
My history teachers, for inspiring me to look at the past.
My science teachers, for opening my eyes to the space-time continuum.
George Lucas, for bringing the world something special.
Microsoft, for their handy technology.
Agape Imaging, for my picture.
My "muses" – the advanced readers.
The editors and publisher, for their assistance in this book.
St. Thomas More Newman Center staff and the 20/30 group.

WARNING! NOT RECOMMENDED FOR ANYONE UNDER THE AGE OF 14.

PROLOGUE

Let us begin in a world close by, not so long ago…

The classic story of visionary George Lucas' space opera tale begins like the fairy tales of old and has become the modern fairy tale. This saga is the tale of good vs. evil, light and dark, hope vs. fear. The saga of those star warriors, the Skywalkers, is a story that takes place a long time ago, but also right now. Star Wars is your story. But it is also mine.

In the following pages you will read how the saga and others like it have shaped my worldview and reflected the lens of my faith in the almighty God. Jump into this journey with me. But just know, there may be spoilers.

Humanity is the premier race on Earth. We are the most intelligent animals, and our capacity for generosity never ceases to amaze me. Yet at the same time, humans are the most violent beings on the planet. Everywhere there is one group trying to wipe out another. All this brutality is almost enough to make one go crazy.

It is my sworn oath to portray how nothing is without hope despite the sadness. What is the good news you might ask? The Holy Trinity, specifically God. He is an omnipotent loving being who transcends the space-time continuum, capable of executing miracles. Indeed, he created the greatest miracle of all time, the Earth and life itself. Unfortunately, some people think such a thing is impossible. I am here to tell you it is possible using logic (part of the original title of this book). Be prepared for any surprise. I am completely open and honest about extremely sensitive and important issues. Knowledge is power, and I wish to bring the truth out. I know you can handle it. During the writing process, I wanted to know how other people thought. I wanted to think like an atheist, understand how they went through life without knowledge of higher powers. I nearly succeeded. You see, it is easy to blow off God. "He doesn't exist. Darwin knows everything. Humans invented God to fulfill a loss in their soul, a loss which logic cannot fill." It is easy to go with the status quo, be it blind faith or humanism, and not think hard about what reality is. God doesn't want blind faith. It is only through questioning what we believe that our faith grows stronger. I am attempting to explain how life's problems can be solved logically, and how God is real.

Another reason for this endeavor is to answer some questions you might have regarding religion. This book is not only for the faithful who may be questioning the meaning of the universe but also for atheists wondering what the hype is about. If I could save one person's soul or bring happiness to someone needing it, then this was worth it.

One thing this isn't going to be is a sort-of salacious tell-all. After all, it has been a truism that I never had good stories. My life has been rather boring since my birth in late 1989, all things considered. Although there was that one time I got off on the wrong exit and took the carpool on an impromptu tour of the east side of the city. The ones in my head don't make for compelling narratives, of that I am sure.

I wrote this prologue, but an epilogue would not be relevant. Sorry. If you feel you must have some sort of ending, read the Review. Quick note on the timing. The unofficial cutoff is January 2019, with a start date circa 1999. I am not ready to tell the rest of the story.

Chapter 1

Who Am I?

"You failed, your Highness. I am a Jedi, like my father before me."[1]

When I first saw Star Wars: Episode VI Return of the Jedi® so many years ago, I know I had seen something special. The whole universe drew me in with its awesome battles, strong heroes, and good vs. evil themes. It is a modern fairy tale in the vein of the tales of old. That is one reason for its enduring legacy in the popular zeitgeist and in my own life.

I truly fell in love with it with the Special Editions and grew up with the prequels. And I do love the sequels. I am one of those fans who love all the films, in fact. I also have a deep love of the expanded universe, being a completionist.

Now, I have to ask, who am I? That is a good question. In fact, who are all of us? Such questions frequently run through my head.

When I was writing this over the last dozen years, I joked it was my autobiography. Logically, though, it is true, from a certain point of view—the words in this book come from my experiences. Still, I should include a section answering self-aware questions. I am Thomas Myers, born six weeks early on November 17, 1989. I went to St. Cecilia elementary school for nine years, and then I switched to a public high school called Central Crossing. Later I went to The Ohio State University and completed a second degree later online through DeVry University; and am now working on yet another degree through Arizona State University online as well. The constants in my life are God, my family, and being a nerd. I was born and raised in the Roman Catholic faith. Also, I basically run my life using Excel spreadsheets. There is a lot of fun in being a completionist when it comes to media or collecting. And if you're curious, my favorite food is fried chicken.

I am also a confused young man struggling to find his place in this world after a lonely childhood. I had a lonely childhood for several reasons, including a conscious decision to be a loner. I don't wish to blame my parents, but their complicity in my choice is undeniable. When I was younger, I was frequently ostracized for having a speech impediment.

When I was alone, I relied on my intellect. I had a group of imaginary friends, based mostly on Star Wars®, Robotech®, and Mobile Suit Gundam Wing® characters, and many plastic building pieces. I had many grand adventures. I even 'married' Leia Organa. These fantasies lasted for some time, up to my freshman year of high school. Perhaps because I spent so much time in my own head, I never learned how to interact well with others. To this day I prefer to stay in and play games rather than venture out to something new. And although I am a creative type, as evidenced by this, I certainly have trouble sticking to a deadline.

My Seventh Grade Spaghetti Dinner scarred me for life. I spilled a plate of spaghetti on a customer, so I did not want to be a waiter. I bumped into my priest, so now I have confidence issues around authority figures—I have an irrational thought I am always being judged. I also generally made a nuisance of myself, further increasing my shyness. One of my main problems is shyness. I feel as though I have nothing to say to people, or if I do, they will judge it and hate me. Yes, I know it is irrational. My counselor told me I just need practice. For now, I feel much more comfortable on the computer.

A friend of mine back in high school told me he had this theory. To him, I was socially inept and appeared to have a social disorder, but I was remarkably intelligent and in tune with reality. He says the Thomas Myers presented to the outside world doesn't exist, and it is a cover-up for something. He said I must be making a choice to be like that.

He is more correct than he thinks (recent events have truly born this out). How much? I am not sure. I do know I never made a concerted effort to change, and I am covering feelings of inadequacy. Still, I am working on turning the 'fake' Thomas into the real one.

Over time, I developed a passion for learning and logic, something I enjoy to this day. I became obsessed with continuity, reading everything I could get my hands on regarding numerous pop-culture franchises. Having plenty of free time allowed me to sit and think and question the universe. I recently decided what the secret to happiness is: finding fulfillment. I dedicated my life to bringing happiness to others. I do that best by sending out e-mails to a myriad of people full of applicable philosophy or posting on Facebook.

I took four years of Honors English in high school and developed a trenchant wit, surely noticeable in the text. Through other classes, I realized I had a passion for sociology, history, and science. I came to school with my dashing good looks and my near-encyclopedic knowledge of pop culture. Those things cannot be learned.

It is worth mentioning my life is full of contradictions. For instance, I suffered from depression because of my loneliness, but I am a consummate optimist. At least, I am optimistic when I am not overwhelmed. During my senior year, my greatest accomplishment was getting a Congressional nomination to the United States Naval Academy, but I had trouble finding a job. Of course, by the summer, things had changed. The Academy sent a rejection letter and I was hired at Kroger as a Fuel Clerk. In addition, I have had a speech problem for much of my life; in grade school I was a social outcast. In high school, though, it didn't matter. My friends voted me the Fall Homecoming King my senior year. If I seem hypocritical at any time, I apologize. All I can say is the trait runs heavy in my family, and all humans make mistakes. The key is to learn from them (something I have trouble doing). I am also strongly opinionated.

Since I have found fulfillment by helping others, I decided to make it my primary career goal. I believe the secret to happiness is finding your passion. I am now attending college and am part of the Navy Reserve Officer Training Corps. If I stay with the program, after graduation I will be commissioned as an ensign. As I am sitting here writing this in my fourth week, I am reflecting on how poorly I am adjusting to life at college. I must get up early every day for ROTC, and I am exhausted. I am expected to be in great shape, but I never played a sport, so in essence I am starting from scratch. In addition, I was unprepared for the workload and the complete freedom I have. Still, college can be full of amazing experiences. For those of you who have not been to college, life is all about choices—healthy lifestyles, partying, watching a movie outside with dozens of others, and so on. My best advice for success is to never forget your goals. It is easy to get lost in today's world, but it is important to remember who you are and what you want. I also remember my debts. I owe so much to my family; I would not be here today without them.

As a matter of fact, I did not take long to start making a difference. On 21 October 2008, I participated in the International Pro-Life Day of Silent Solidarity, an event where participants took a vow of silence to protest abortion. It was a successful day. I had several pro-choicers stop me and say they respected me for standing up for what I believe in. It has been proven life begins at conception, when the sperm meets and fertilizes the eggs. What a woman carries is special; all human life is special. 50,000,000 children have been murdered since January 22, 1973 (Pro-Life) [2]. A terrifying statistic. Abortion is an epidemic (Forced Abortions). Of course, a choice between the life of the mother and the life of a baby is no choice. The mother takes priority. I simply know the decision to just get rid of an 'inconvenient' pregnancy is wrong. We as a society worship sex. Maybe we would have fewer abortions if teenage boys were not screwing everything in sight. Or if culture did not view women as sex objects and women see a need to have a 'perfect body' to be loved. Read chapter 3 for an in-depth look at sexual morality.

Getting back to me, as a politician, I know I can help others. I originally decided to pursue a piloting career in the United States Navy, though. Becoming a pilot requires you to be top in everything, so I centered my life on this ambitious goal. Even after I found I could not be a pilot, as I lack 20/20 vision, I never saw a reason to re-evaluate the way I do things, so I am still a top student, seeking numerous extracurricular activities. I even managed to become an Eagle Scout. Still, my involvement has served me well. I am still planning on joining the Navy after college, doing diplomatic work. Actually, all Naval Officers must take their first tour of duty on a ship, a submarine, or an aircraft squadron, or as Marine Infantry Officer. I plan on being a Surface Warfare Officer, which means I will be on a surface ship. After my first tour, I want to transfer and become a Foreign Affairs Officer, which is a type of diplomat. After 20 years, I am retiring, and in 2036 I am running for president. Or, I will stay in the Navy; wherever I feel I will be most successful. The road less taken, after all.

Some things I will never understand. Mirror Lake Jump is one such thing. For those of you who are not a Buckeye, over in the University's Oval we have a pond called Mirror Lake. The Thursday before the Michigan-OSU game, students (mostly first years) jump into the freezing water late at night. 2008 was an interesting event. In the midst of a light snowfall, hordes of people were in the lake in a variety of clothing styles. One could hear the Buckeye Battle cry everywhere. On another note, more than a few were in an altered state of conscious. But that is not the point. It is an odd tradition where people act out; we had flags, costumes, even

an inflatable beer can. Oh yes. People were swimming, and there was a canoe for a while. Dozens of police officers were just standing there watching. The whole Michigan Week was exciting.
At this point, I am happy with my life. If only I could stop procrastinating. I feel I am truly blessed. All my friends are passionate people. I am at a wonderful university. I have three wonderful roommates, Matthew, Mark, and Luke (I changed their names for security purposes). My parents have given me everything I've ever needed. And I am loved by God who is outside our reality.

Flash forward about 19 months, which is how long I put this off. Still at OSU, and now with three new roommates. The room relationships with them have proven to be far more interesting. Actually, did not attend Mirror Lake Jump this year. For personal reasons, I have left the NROTC program. Yet I gained something more profound. I found a job on campus, working in a Dining Hall. I work with really great people. In fact, I was given the chance to become a manager. Having re-evaluated my life, I definitely want to work overseas for the State Department, and maybe run for president later. And still loved by God. Needless to say, the Navy plan did not work out. As for the other part--still working on it.

One thing I do every day is listen to music or podcasts (90s pop). I also make sure to visit Wookieepedia®, the Star Wars fandom site where I help make lists and run a Project. And play video games as often as possible (Ace Combat 5®, Command & Conquer: Tiberian Sun®, and Star Wars: The Force Unleashed®).

Flash forward again…a long time. I put off this writing for a variety of reasons. During that time, I went through a lot of struggles. In the meantime, I was diagnosed as being on the autism spectrum disorder, which in hindsight puts a lot of this into more clarity. One good thing is an encyclopedic knowledge. I like to think it doesn't affect my day-to-day life, but it really does. It turns things into a cloud sometimes. It isn't easy, but I make the best of it that I can. Some of these struggles put perspective into how everything happens for a reason. The plan hasn't worked out, and in many ways, I am still figuring it out, but I am content to be on God's path.

CHAPTER 2

What it Means to be Christian

"You are nothing! A scavenger girl is no match for the power in me! I am all the Sith!"[3]

The Jedi Order is said to have protected the noble Galactic Republic for over 1,000 generations.[4] They are peacekeepers, who carry their traditional weapon, the lightsaber. They use their powers for defense, and not for aggression, and show compassion for their fellow beings. Before they were struck down by their eternal enemy, the dark side-following Order of the Sith Lords. But with the Skywalker legacy, they ultimately triumphed. To be a Jedi is to be a power for good.

As I hope I made clear in the last chapter, that is something I hope to do.

In our own world, 2000 years ago a star appeared over the town of Bethlehem. The stellar anomaly heralded the fulfillment of ancient Jewish Scripture, who prophesized the savior, the Son of God. The star marked the place of the Messiah's birth, in a simple manger. Jesus Christ the Messiah was born to two parents, Mary and Joseph. For more information read the Gospels, especially John. Another anomaly in Jesus' birth is the fact his mother Mary was a virgin. A birth without sex? Gasp! Actually, today such an event is not unheard of. In vitro fertilization does not involve sexual intercourse. And there are a number of virgin births in mythology. I'm looking at you, Athena. The question is not whether Mary was a virgin, but what was the exact moment of procreation? I know the Holy Spirit implanted Jesus' genetic information into Mary, merging it with her egg. When did this happen? Traditionally, it would have been when Mary said yes to the Angel Gabriel, before she said yes, or on the way to see her cousin Elizabeth. Our name, Christian, signifies we are followers of the Christ, who awakened us the knowledge of the Holy Trinity. Until He came, it was just God, according to tradition.

Anyway, back to the theme of the chapter. To be Christian is to believe in the Word of God, as given by Jesus to the world. Yes, He was Jewish, but his followers became Christian due to their belief in Jesus as savior and Messiah. It is a complicated matter. Judaism is the Father of Christianity, and the first monotheist religion, or belief in only one god. Yet it is not by our faith alone that we are saved. James 2:17 explains that even so faith, if it hath not works, is dead. God asks us to help our fellow humans. It is the least we can do, considering how He created the world.

When Jesus died on the Cross, it was to save us from sin and fulfill the sacred Covenant made to humankind. We call him the Good Shepherd for this, as he tends to His flock and washes away their wrongdoing with the blood of the lamb (figuratively speaking). One of the pastors at the Church I attend now likes to quote a scholar about the ineffable mystery of Jesus becoming fully human (as well as fully divine) and walking among us.[5]

This bears repeating. It is awesome that our God sent Jesus

down for us to remove our sins. And from a historical perspective, Jesus was radical in just about every sense of the word. The Jewish people were prophesized and expected a Messiah in the military sense to free them from the shackles of Roman rule. Instead, they received a Messiah who came to fulfill the covenant with all humankind, who said "For what does it profit a man, if he shall gain the whole world, and lose his own soul"? (Mark 8:36). Furthermore, he took his preaching's straight to the people and decried the hypocrisy of the Sanhedrin, the main leadership of the Jewish faith.

Love was his message. Love for your neighbor and for yourself. The message gets lost in the miasma of the world today, but it truly needs to be on the lips of every Christian. And not just on our lips, but in our actions as well. Live each moment for God.

These days, our personal sacrifices do not necessarily mean you have to mortgage your home and give it to the Red Cross, or work in a soup kitchen every day for a year. The Holy Spirit gives everyone unique gifts to succeed. We are expected to use these gifts in the best way possible. Personally, you hold one of my gifts in your hands.

I am a member of the Roman Catholic church. Little "c" catholic means universal, which means it is consistent and widespread. For the cliff notes version of what we believe, please see the Nicene Creed, a main prayer finalized over the centuries which we recite during the mass.

Again, human nature seems to be hard. All work and no play? Take heart, the life we have chosen is a blessed life. There are many good things in life. Jesus has died so that we may have life to the fullest, or so we are told in John 10:10. God has given us the promise of eternal bliss in heaven. Heaven is a spot outside the space-time continuum where God resides and the souls of all faithful reside, singing eternal praise to God. In a closer location, here amongst ourselves, we can see a little bit of heaven. It was the Holy Trinity who gave us all the ability to love, because we were created in His image.

Much has been made about the Seven Deadly Sins, the chief activities that we see are lacking in the good. Sin is any action that separates us from God, whether large or small, omission or commission. These Deadly Sins are tempered by the Seven Virtues, which are basically Good Habits in our daily lives: chastity, temperance, charity, diligence, patience, kindness, and humility.[6] Jesus also gave us the Beatitudes as aspirational behavior.

Some of you may be wondering what I may be blabbering about when I mention the Holy Trinity. You may have heard of just God and His Son Jesus. There is a third Entity, the Holy Spirit. He is the bringer of life. Saint Augustine once heard God say to him that he is no closer to explaining God than counting sand on a beach. Yet I will attempt to. I have several hundred years' advantage on Saint Augustine.

Catholicism is also a monotheist religion. We believe in one God — with three parts. Think of your mother. She is one person, but simultaneously three parts — wife, mother, and whatever her job is. Dante Alighieri explained the Holy Trinity as three circles within one. Each part has a specific duty. God the Father is the creator of heaven and Earth. God the Son (Jesus) walked on Earth as both man and God. How this is possible is the greatest mystery of our faith, and any attempts to explain it are correspondingly incomplete. The Holy Spirit gives us life and grace. Grace is a special gift.

Back in the old days, English leaders once tried to trap Saint Joan of Arc in a scholarly trap. They asked her if she was in God's grace, for the knowledge of grace is beyond us. She replied, "If I am not in the state of grace, may God put me there; and if I am, may God so keep me."[7] A very adroit response, and one that gets to the heart of it.

From this point on, the author will refer to each one by their individual identity; all three will be known as the Holy Trinity.

One the eve of His death, Jesus shared the Passover supper with His disciples. He broke the bread and said, "this is My body," and of the wine, "this is My blood. It will be shed for you, in fulfillment of scripture. Do this in memory of me" (Luke 22:19). Since then, receiving Communion in memory of Him during the mass has become an imperative for the faithful. The nature of the Eucharist, the bread and body are the greatest mystery in Catholic dogma. In a process known as transubstantiation, the Eucharist becomes the actual body and blood of Jesus. The priest is responsible for the prayers necessary for the transformation. I have been honored to act as an altar server, assisting the priest with mass, at multiple points in my life.

Saint Augustine of Hippo (a declared Doctor of the Church and all-around interesting guy) had a lot to say on the specialty of this back in the 300s AD: "If you receive well, you are what you have received. Since you are the body of Christ and His members, it is your mystery that you receive. Be, therefore, members of Christ, that your 'Amen' may be true. Be what you see and receive what you are."[8] That is a very adroit calling. We must always act as if the Eucharist is something Holy.

Some Protestant congregations believe in a process known as consubstantiation, where the Eucharist does not turn into the body and blood, but Jesus is still present in the bread and wine, considering His words to us in the Gospels.

Christianity has its roots in Judaism. Jesus the Son of God was a Jew. We took our monotheist dogma from the Jews, and the idea of Sabbath, the day of rest. For them it is on Saturday; the Christian Sabbath is Sunday, which in Egyptian Mythology was put aside to the Sun God Ra. Jews are truly monotheistic, believing in one God. Our God.

Christians have a mortal Enemy: Satan. He was created as one with the angels in the order of beings. It is often said that the universe has a balance, a natural dichotomy of good and evil. Such as in Star Wars' The Force. Our Catholic view is a lot more nuanced. We take the view that "Evil has no positive nature; but the loss of good has received the name 'evil.' Or rather, that which is evil is a matter of lacking the good.[9] That is the Augustinian view of evil. I seem to be quoting him a lot here.

Satan is dedicated to stealing our souls from God. He is a great deceiver. CS Lewis, the man responsible for the Chronicles of Narnia, wrote a book from a demon's perspective, detailing the ways he corrupts humans (Lewis).[10] It is a scary process, ranging from whispers to full-on interference designed to twist our thoughts and lead us into temptation. But God is with is, and he is our shepherd. Vigilance, faith, hope, and love are the tools we have that fight against these malicious influences.

It is a popular misconception that people of faith are just blind sheep. That is so far from the truth. Our faith is "suprarational", which means goes beyond the plain logic and inclusive of it. Indeed, God is the Logos, or reason itself. At least for me, I believe because it is right. There is a beauty to our faith, which adopts a sort of "both and", not either or. We Christians want to see the good in things, especially the transcendentals of truth, beauty, and goodness.

The framework of these transcendentals informs our worldview. We seek the truth of reality and act in relation to the truth. We admire beauty, which can evoke wonder and delight. We also recognize and explore goodness; one definition of which is the perfection of being. Objective goodness, therefore, is logically something that adheres to its nature and purpose.

Now, preaching the gospel, the Word of God, is the quintessential Christian activity. It is our calling, born of scripture. It is a storied history, described in Luke chapter 10, with the sending of the 72 followers. It is quite a bit different, and arguably more difficult, in today's world. At the same time, modern technology should be an opportunity for greater reach. Archbishop Fulton Sheen, a Servant of God, had an approachable and enlightened television program in the middle portion of the last century, which should be the gold standard of modern evangelization.[11] This work is our great commission. Jesus called us to go where the people are.

I want you to seriously think of something. Humans are not like animals because we are self-aware. Why? God made us that way and gave us our souls. Logically, we should not be self-aware and have an appreciation for art. God must exist to give us these, because evolution did not.

I could go on for hours about how great God and His gifts are, but I think you get the idea. This is my way of evangelizing and speaking my truth.

It's not easy to be Christian. Jesus tells us we have a cross to carry. In this day, it seems our cross is simply to be a follower of Christ. Being faithful is looked down on; we are made fun of for believing in something without proof, not to mention an afterlife. They say humans are only of the world, a product of evolution. There is no God. To the naysayers, I say, well, just continue to read. Anyway, our cross is a burden we must carry. My cross is overcoming my secret, revealed in the next chapter.

One more note on Jesus' work. As part of His ministry was making it accessible and was fond of parables. One of them, about the household being ready for the bridegroom, teaches us to be ready for the moment of His return. He also admonished us to "love thy neighbor as thyself" (Mark 22:39), and he made a point about laying down one's life for another.

Kind of how like the story of one Rey Skywalker worked out. More about Star Wars® and love later…

CHAPTER 3

Sexual Purity

"I love you." "I know."[12]

There's not a whole lot that the galaxy far, far away has to say on matters of the heart. Just that there are...interesting love stories. A hint of destiny and the will of The Force. And the Jedi Code calls for compassion for all living things.

As for our world, Mary, the mother of Jesus was considered to be a virgin her entire life, as was her Son. As a community, we are called to follow their example. It is a disheartening trend in today's world of a cheapening of love and sexuality. There is a reason God created endorphins (released into the brain during intercourse). Humans need an incentive to mate because nine months later out pops a helpless infant. Endorphins are what have sex feel so good.

The sole reason for sex is procreation. It is not for a teenage football player do to waste time on a Saturday evening! There is too much risk of pregnancy, not to mention the risk of sexual transmitted infection if either one had a prior encounter.

Sex is the greatest expression of love you can give, and it is a beautiful thing. You are saying 'I love you so much I want to create new life with you.' If you wait to have sex until marriage, it will be a whole lot more fun to explore its joys with someone with whom you will spend the rest of your life with.

There is a slight difference between virginity and chastity. Virginity means you have not engaged in sexual intercourse. Chastity means you treat sex in a responsible manner, and that means more than just being a virgin. All sex is off-limits, including anal and oral. Anything which cheapens or disrespects sex is bad, outside of its proper context in the sacrament of marriage.

Pornography is an evil business. It exploits women, men and sometimes even children. Such images have sex cheap and that is unacceptable. I should know. For much of my life, I was addicted to those images. It happened by accident. I was curiously exploring, and discovered I liked it. Believe me when I say pornography is a problem. I managed to put the past behind me, turn off the computer, and look to the future. It has not been easy, but I made a decision to be chaste. Like all addictions, the key is to replace it with another positive feeling. For me, it was spending time on the computer — away from sex videos on YouTube (I went to positive fan sites instead) and working on my life's work. Prostitution does a similar thing as porn, only worse, since you are giving away your body with someone else. The sex trade is the new slavery. It is sickening. Masturbation cheapens sex, but if one cannot keep their hormones in check, they are advised to masturbate. It is the lesser of two evils, because it is the same thing, only without the risk of pregnancy. You may ask why masturbation is bad in the first place. "Everyone does it, and you just said to go ahead and do it." Here's why. Masturbation (Greek-to disturb your penis) is wrong because you are disrespecting not only your body's natural functions but also disrespects whomever you are thinking about when you are stimulating yourself. You love that person for their body, not their personality. Of course, you don't have to be male to 'jack off.' What I said applies to both men and women.

We as a society are contemptibly bland. I've spent much time on YouTube, watching music videos of my favorite pop songs. I take the time to read the comments. Consistently, they all follow the same subject on each video. Either they are sexual references, or they are praising/ hating the artists. People actually try to be insulting as possible, especially on the religious videos. One example is the commentators on the Hang On Sloopy[13] .talked about how the dancer lacked a bra. This is a problem in our society. We are promoting a view of beauty which runs contrary to everything God teaches us. Beauty is inside us; yet our culture alienates those who do not meet a certain standard and forces many to change their body to conform.

Ironically, I am still a virgin. I am dedicated to preserving the special gift that I can only give to one person. Besides, with the way things always turn out I would probably catch gonorrhea from anyone other than my wife. Furthermore, I respect my friends too much to engage in a one night stand. I could not act as if nothing happened; now I have shared something special with that person. Actually, I don't wish to get married. I feel I am called to the single life. I feel there is no room for anyone else in my life. Although, since I set this book aside, I have decided to pursue a dating relationship.

The reason I mentioned gonorrhea is because it is the most common STD. If you engage in casual sex, you should get tested. Promiscuous love-making should always include condoms. Abstinence is 100% effective against pregnancy, but condoms are the next best thing. I may be against promiscuous sex, but I would be misguided not to give out information which could be helpful. I am not naïve enough to think young people are not having sex. Heck, I am in college. I know they are. In fact, each room in my dorm had to agree on a signal for when we are with someone. One of the reasons I am so disgusted with immoral sex is because I was verbally molested when I was in grade school. I had someone say he wanted to "milk me." Yes, I am a guy. No, I am not gay. I don't think he is, either. It was just another way to make fun of me. Of course, I have long since forgiven him. I just provide this information, so you have a complete picture.

Also, Pope John Paull II's groundbreaking encyclical Humanae Vitae[14] is the last word in sexual morality.

CHAPTER 4

On Relations

"I think our lives are about to be destroyed anyway. I truly..., deeply... love you and before we die, I want you to know."[15]

The Force is said to penetrate and flow between all living things and bind the galaxy together.[16] Maybe that is a metaphor for what love is.

I don't profess to understand intimacy; I can only give you my opinion, especially since finding love while autistic is…difficult. Love is when you are willing to put your partner's needs above your own. That being said, marriage is an equal partnership. Fights will happen, but the important thing to do is to forgive and move on. Part of being an equal partnership involves compromising for the good of the other. As well as recognizing and celebrating the aforementioned transcendentals.

The Book of Genesis tells how woman was made from the side of man. So, when they are joined in marriage, two become one again. That is a metaphorical way of looking at it, but also a very beautiful way. Declaring one's love and commitment to their spouse is meant to be.

Jesus is married to the Church. It is for this reason priests do not get married — they are married to the Church in the same way. Their commitment is unshakeable. Similarly, marriage between two individuals is an unbreakable commitment. Yet many people choose to end it. Many people divorce; statistics show 50% of marriages fail. This is a sad act. Yet are there times when a divorce is absolutely necessary? Yes, when one spouse does something to upset the balance or the marriage was done on an unstable foundation.

Having a divorce any other time and people are cheapening marriage. Or worse, they use a divorce to take revenge on one another. People have many examples to look to — and you know who they are — their marriages last mere days, or they have their own TV shows trying to find a mate.

I tell you; this is not how it is done. Love cannot be found in reality TV. I decry their examples.

On another note, the government does not have the right to declare what love is, and in fact none of us do. If people of the same gender want to fall in love, who are we to stop them? They are people with hopes and fears, just like us so-called 'normal' people.

All humans are created equal. This great country was founded on that statement and it holds true the world over. The founders got the idea from John Locke. Human life is an incalculably great item. Seven billion of us have worth. Yet need I mention everything wrong with what we do with each other? Gangs, religious strife, rape, etc. I can't take back thousands of years of violence, but maybe I can do something for the future. We can start by reaching out to the people around us; even a simple smile can raise someone's spirits. On an ironic twist, smiling releases endorphins, the neurotransmitters involved in another biological function. Smiling (and laughing) really does make you feel better.

On a more serious note, I need to address a terrible issue.

Humans continue to kill each other. Not everyone believes humans are made equal. At this time, over a million people lie dead in Africa because of hate. It was pointed out to me in my AP English IV class imperialism caused the underlying issues. Some say we were wrong to go down and impose our culture, and religious missionary work was a grave error, and that when we were down in Africa giving aid, we shoved religion down their throats. They did not have a choice but to convert.

Which is not a good argument; missionary work is inherently peaceful. Even if they are correct about the negativity or not, missionary work in general has been glorified. Personally, going to other cultures and helping them improve conditions, bringing plumbing and new crops, for instance, is a wonderful thing. We can a better world in the future. As Christians, we are called to spread the word of God to all people. Missionary work is, therefore, the duty of all.

What is a nation? They are a collection of people, living in borders. States have the legitimate use of force. Is patriotism a bad thing? No, this abstract concept stems from a love of country. As long as this love does not interfere with the worship, it is fine. Indeed, patriotism can be a positive thing; being a patriot incites civic responsibility and fosters a care for fellow humans.

We all know patriotism can be a bad thing when manipulated to one's own agenda. I won't digress this time into the myriad examples.

There is a beautiful and uniquely human act known as forgiveness. Can the zebra forgive the lion when its throat is ripped out? No, that is an act of nature. Forgiveness is necessary in this world. It helps us keep hate from forming in our hearts. Does forgiveness mean there can be no justice or punishment? Of course not. Forgiveness does not mean we forget, only move on. Sometimes it is even necessary for society to separate us from the rest of society and help us take responsibility for our actions. Overall, though, people deserve a second chance.

Men and women are often at odds. Men have long subjugated the opposite gender. That needs to stop. Women are just as capable as men in any task. I am calling for equality for all women. For instance, why shouldn't they be allowed into combat? Look at the new Battlestar Galactica. The best pilot, Starbuck, is a woman! Not to mention Princess Leia led an entire Rebellion. Also, Women would make wonderful priests. They will bring new ideas and new strengths, revitalizing the order. How could this be bad?

Pope John Paul II talked about how we each have a part to play. Women must be restricted to the nunnery because they are better at prayer. Hogwash! We need more men to act as friars anyways. Recently the Episcopalians even had a lesbian bishop for a short time.

Historically, women have not been accepted into the priesthood because Jesus did not take any women apostles. It was a cultural trend that women were pushed to the side. Yet His best friend, Mary Magdalene, was a woman. She might even have been a prostitute (there is controversy regarding whether or not she was). There is also the issue about how male priests are married to the church, and for a woman to be a priest implies a wrong relationship. Yet, is not Jesus THE Church? So, for a male priest to be married to the church implies a male-male partnership. The point is, service to the church is open to all, regardless of gender, age, or race. This is the twenty-first century, for crying out loud.

Let's see if we can do something about the world's problems. The answer is out there. The Law of Conservation of Energy state "energy cannot be created or destroyed, only change form."[17] Unfortunately, it is impossible to achieve a 100/100 ratio of energy conversion. Energy is lost to friction. It is impossible to achieve a perpetual motion machine. That means although we can conserve energy, it will always be lost/transformed. We need intelligent solutions to the energy crisis. God granted us this world to share, not hoard and waste.

We are taught from a young age to obey authority; not for power's sake but only for our well-being. Of course, as we grow older, so does the greater responsibility to obey authority. Sometimes, though, authority pushes the boundary. They crave power. That is a problem. Of course, we are obligated to take power from those who are misusing it.

When in the course of human events it becomes necessary for one people to dissolve the political bands which have connected them with another and to assume among the powers of the earth, the separate and equal station to which the Laws of Nature and of Nature's God entitle them, a decent respect to the opinions of humankind requires that they should declare the causes which impel them to the separation (Declaration of Independence).

Those words are of great comfort. Our forebears stood up to evil and prevailed. I still believe that we can do the same.

Let's talk redemption. It is a central theme of the Star Wars Saga, and necessary in Christian lives. Can one good deed make up for a lifetime of hate and anger? In God's eyes; human justice calls for an exchange of punishment for redemption. Any sane person is capable of turning aside. Anakin Skywalker made his choices out of love and was redeemed for the same reason.

CHAPTER 5

Psychology

"You and the Naboo form a symbiont circle. What happens to one of you will affect the other. You must understand this."[18]

"The Force can have a strong influence on the weak-minded."[19] There are no Jedi Mind Tricks in the real world, so it is up to us to work out how we can navigate our relationships. Probably a good thing, as the potential for misuse is kinda strong. But we can still use our knowledge to get into another's head and understand them. Walk a mile in their shoes, etc.

We are animals. Literally. The only thing which sets us apart from the beasts is our self-awareness, the ability to see us ourselves as "I." We have instincts, just as much as an ant, albeit stronger. The ability to survive is second-to-none. We may not be physically strong like a lion, but we can use our intellect to escape. We are aided by our endocrine system, which in times of crisis sends signals to the brain and opens up our adrenal gland, flooding our system with adrenaline. The neurotransmitter gives us a temporary boost, and we must take a split-second to decide what to do with the energy boost. This is known as the fight-or-flight response.

The power of the human mind is a wonderful thing. Thank God for self-awareness. The facility to use our imagination is breathtaking, bringing us to other lands, etc. Anyway, people see what they want to see, which can be good or bad. We can convince ourselves to overlook minor transgressions, or even bigger ones.

Much has been talked about folly. I think why we need to laugh at ourselves is to remind us how we can't take things too seriously. For after all, "I did not, like other infants, come crying into the world, but perked up, and laughed immediately in my mother's face."5-2 Folly is telling what is obviously false and pretending it to be true, just for a laugh. Imitation is the highest form of flattery. Some people take folly and imitation too far, making folly at someone else's expense. They do it for several reasons, perhaps out of a desire to make themselves feel better by making others feel bad. Power can be a drug.

We can even look away from witnessing a crime scene because we do not want to get involved. I've heard it said, "All it takes for evil to triumph is for good people to do nothing." What is evil, exactly? And what is sin? The Spanish word for "without" is "sin." Perhaps that is a good explanation. Sin is an act "without" love. When we sin, we are lacking in love for God, and depending on the circumstances, lacking in love for anyone else.

Why is human nature the same the world over? Sociologists since Aristotle have debated the topic. Some see the development of individuality as nature vs. nurture, i.e. ingrained instincts vs. our childhood environment. It is the author's opinion we are not born with a tabula rasa, as John Locke hypothesized. Tabula rasa means blank slate[20] and we are born with nothing and shaped by what happens in our life. No, human instincts are based in our DNA. These instincts include not only the flight-or-fight response but the drive to survive, no matter what.

This drive is present in every other animal and is partly why humans are animals. Alone or in small groups, humans will do anything to get on top. At our basest levels, we are vile creatures.

Fortunately, we are hard-wired to be social animals, seeking out relationships with those like us. Society develops through our interactions with others, and society brings us morality and religion.

Many atheists see God as a fabrication. Evidence points to this because many people are not truly faithful. They give lip-service at best but expect God to come to them in their moments of need. This suggests God only exists to serve our whims, or to give comfort in time of need, bringing light to our dreary lives to say there is something waiting for us in the afterlife. To some, the belief there is no afterlife is a comforting thought. To them, they don't have to worry about anyone but themselves.

The truth is, God is no more a fabrication than a rainbow. He created us, and gave us souls, and the actions we do in this life decide where our souls will reside (more in later chapters). God is more than a crutch, as atheists call him. God wants us to offer our problems up to him. He loves us, but he is not a crutch. He gives us the gifts we need to succeed. The Holy Trinity is everywhere, watching over us.

Jesus had to have been real. No apostle of God, such as Saints Peter, Paul, and Stephen would make up his story. Their works prove they are part of something higher than themselves. Many historical documents exist outside of the Bible describing their lives. Peter was the first Pope of the Catholic Church. Paul was imprisoned by the Romans. Stephen was the first martyr, stoned to death by heretics after he was preaching about Jesus.

CHAPTER 6

The Bible

"Luminous beings are we, not this crude matter."[21]

The closest thing the galaxy far, far away has to a unifying book of records is the Jedi Code, passed to generations of Jedi. Look it up sometime; I've got it posted next to my desk. As I said above, the Jedi are a force for good. The metaphysics of the saga may be different from our own, but we can learn a lot from it.

The Bible is our sacred Scripture, our Book of Common Prayer (Anglican), so to speak. Actually, the preceding sentence is not exact. The Catechism explains in-depth dogma, whereas the Bible is the Word of God made manifest. Every word in Scripture comes directly or indirectly from God. Its development process was long and complex, but Christian scholars agree prophets from the past were 'inspired' by the Holy Spirit to write it. The Spirit probably appeared to them in dreams.

It is worth noting the difference between the New and Old

Testaments. They are both crucial to our life, especially since the OT gave us the Ten Commandments. The OT chronicles God's creation of a chosen people (The 12 tribes of Jerusalem), unto whom He will give His only begotten Son, Jesus. The New Testament accounts Jesus' mission and that of his apostles. The two Testaments act in conjunction to explore God's plan for humanity and the course of the sacred Covenant.

The Bible consists of many stories. In the fourth century, church officials decided what would be considered canon, or the official set of books. They established the apocrypha, or what is not considered to be part of the Bible. This was before the discovery of the Dead Sea Scrolls. They are apocryphal, but still very useful for historical reference. There are also Gnostic Gospels, or books written by authors who may or may not be the people they say they are. The Gnostic Gospels appeared centuries after Jesus' death, and were often associated with heretical groups. For instance, the Gospel of Mary Magdalene is Gnostic. Interestingly, the Bible multi-genre, incorporating historical accounts, prayers, and even love poems. This in turn means its sum is greater than its parts.

In the New Testament, the four Gospels form the core of it and chronicle Jesus' mission down here on earth. Matthew, Mark, Luke, and John are the four writers who either met Jesus Himself or His disciples. Their works have been passed down through the centuries. And they resonate today, and in each of us.

Reading the Bible should be a routine practice for people of faith; indeed, many households make it part of their day. It is by reading scripture that we come to a fuller understanding of the Word of God and our relationship to the Holy Trinity. That practice serves to unite Catholics in all nations, as they go through the daily readings and have done so the same as our forebears.

I would say now that my favorite verse comes from Matthew's Gospel, Chapter 5, verse 13. "You are the salt of the earth: but if the salt has lost his savor, wherewith shall it be salted?" I think it boils down to the essence of what it means to be faithful. We are bound to this earth to do good works. The old mainstay John 3:16 is also a good one. And the Psalms are very beautiful poems. The Acts of the Apostles were written at a specific time to a specific audience but speak to us even today.

I shouldn't have to say it, but one thing it should not be taken as is a scientific textbook. It is the Word of God, yes, but not an in-depth analysis on creation.

The impact of the Bible is undeniable. Some call its fiction. Some read every word as coming from the mouth of God. I was taught in school the Book of Genesis serves as a metaphor for the creation of the world. It should not take God 24 hours to fill the oceans. It took millions of years as the Earth cooled and comets melted into rain. Neither should the Book of Revelation be taken literally. It offers symbolism for the end of the world. See chapter 11 for an in-depth explanation.

CHAPTER 7

Scientific Advancements

"The Force can have a strong influence on the weak-minded."[22]

One of the manifestations of The Force in the Skywalker family is a preternatural piloting ability. And there are so, so many cool ships in the saga for them to fly. I am not ashamed to note that I have memorized the stats of the Rebel Alliance's X-wing ship, a truly beautiful craft. Lucasfilm's design team are some of the most creative people on the planet, that is for sure. The care that the production and design teams put into the films are what drives its success, alongside George's vision.

Our society makes our younglings spend a lot of time in class learning the difference between hypotheses and theories. As it is not something, we use every day, most forget. I will explain them here for educational purposes. A hypothesis is a guess you make before an experiment; a theory is an explanation about recorded data. Both have their places in the Scientific Method, what scientists the world over use to explore our reality. It would be clichéd to quote Spider-Man: "with great power comes great responsibility."[23]

So I will not quote it.

I could fill volumes discussing what humanity has discovered about the universe in the past 300 years. But that would detract from my purpose, so I'll keep it simple. It's time for a little history lesson. 2000 years ago, in the time of Christ, the population was sparse, and technology limited. Even after the Black Plague hit in 1300 AD, humans were a backward society stuck in limbo. The preceding centuries were known as the Dark Ages, because the conservative leaders wanted to keep the status quo. Between 1500 and 1700, the world became reborn, experiencing the Renaissance and Reformation. The arts and sciences flourished, bringing such artists as Shakespeare, Da Vinci, and Descartes.

In the aftermath of this wonderful era came the Industrial Revolution. Countries entered into widespread use of steam power and the assembly line, leading into the twentieth century. Within 70 years, we went from powered flight to visiting our neighbors in space and created advanced technologies like Wikipedia. In addition, never in history had anyone dreamed we could manipulate genetics the way we do now. We are on the threshold of exciting new developments, including a cloned human!

The only things stopping us are 'radical ultraconservatives' like our 43rd president. People like him created 'ethics laws.' The precept behind them get in the way of true advancement. Who knows what we could do without them?

Yes, what could we do without them? I don't know, maybe, clone a human? Hello, these are good laws!!! Cloning a human is the last thing we want to do. It would be an aberration to life itself. Some lines should never be crossed, some stones left unturned. I don't want to cheapen this message, but our culture is replete with what-if stories like Frankenstein or I Am Legend. Humans are not God and we DO NOT have the right to mess with life in such a way.

Stem cell research has proven to be useful in treating chronic illnesses. The problem is, stem cells are harvested from human embryos--the first step in human development. Although unfertilized, the embryos still have potential. In a world that cares about human life, we should not be destroying life just for research. The flip side is, though, stem cells which do not have potential to become life reside in the umbilical cords from babies. Conversely, it would be unethical not to research the 'cord blood' stem cells and other ethically-extracted cells for positive research.

Another interesting scientific topic is computers and artificial intelligence. Every few hours we hear about a new achievement in data storage and processor speed. It is only a matter of time before we can program a computer to outthink a human. At the moment, technology is our servant, making our lives easier and communication instant. Here is a thought. How long before we became the servants of machines? Certainly, when I wrote the proceeding passage, we were barely in the smartphone age and Alexa wasn't a concept.

I don't want to sound like I hate science. I don't—in fact, I find it to be a fascinating pursuit and necessary endeavor. I just take issue with where it is heading. Science and religion are not mutually exclusive. They both have their roles to play in our lives. Science explains how stalactites formed and what a micro black hole is. Religion allows us to communicate with God and receive His blessings and helps us to explain the afterlife.

By far the greatest scientific discovery is not how to split the atom, but the mapping of our Deoxyribonucleic Acid (DNA) strands. The possibilities (and of course, the responsibilities) are endless. The twisted helix rests in every cell in our body and is responsible for our life. 46 chromosomes, 23 from, the sperm and 23 from the egg. When they meet, new life is created. The Star Trek explanation for life is whatever takes in nutrients, replicates, and reacts to its environment is considered to be alive.[24] A chair is not alive. A fertilized gamete is alive, and in about nine months will finish its term in its womb. A fetus has been homo sapiens for nine months at the moment of birth.

CHAPTER 8

Fate

"Only the Sith deal in absolutes. I will do what I must."[25]

Now let us talk about that famous metaphysical concept, The Force. In the words of George Lucas himself on what it actually is, "First, it is a spiritual power that is more god-like than a simple secular moral system. Second, Lucas wanted viewers to connect the Force with the ways we have faith and the supernatural power that seems to control the nature of our universe."[26] Inside the Star Wars universe, the Living Force just about has a mind of its own, able to guide the destiny of a galaxy, and allow good to triumph over evil.

If people have fates, why has it taken so long for the world to change? The answer might be because humanity refuses to accept change. The question and its answer are just one of many I thought about which convinced me to write this book. Events have convinced me many things happen for a reason. We meet our future spouse on the subway; or we hit a stoplight and avoid a deadly crash. God grants us many gifts, and His hand guides us. Sometimes we do not know our purpose until it is too late.

On a more personal note, I fully believe I was born into a family that sponsored loneliness so I can sit and come up with this book, thus bringing hope to your life. I am being serious. I am convinced the reason I am a terrible planner is so I can randomly run into people I know. I try to live my life imitating Jesus, and people notice. Waving hello reminds them of who I am.

This being said, is our life completely planned out? I have truly come to believe that in many ways, it is. God loves us; we are His creation. He wants the best possible life for us, and granted us free will, but guides us toward the best possible outcome of His plan. Stories (most importantly Paradise Lost) say Satan, or Lucifer, was God's right-hand angel. He disagreed with the decision of free will (because humans are animals) and tried to stage a coup. He was thrown out into hell. Is this what really happened? Who knows? But the story certainly offers a new view of sin—not evil but something else.

As I am wrapping this up years after I started, I have truly come to believe that both great and small things happen for a reason. Both the big and little experiences stack up to put us on the path that God wants us to tread. It could be said that a lot of angst comes from not following along this path. Things have a way of pointing us in the right direction toward our best life.

To come to the conclusion about fate, I asked myself questions like, "in the future, if we colonize a planet, is it part of God's will, or will we be permanently affecting the life which will develop in 200,000 years?" "Are we supposed to have giant SUVs on the road, spewing CO_2?" Well, no to the second question, but God wants us to fulfill our potential. As long as we take care of the environment and each other, we can still have comfort items.

CHAPTER 9

The Church

"For over a thousand generations, the Jedi Knights were the guardians of peace and justice in the Old Republic. Before the dark times, before the Empire."[27]

Not too much to say here; the point has been made about the Jedi Order, destiny, and The Force. But it is important to reiterate the heroic journey that Luke Skywalker went on. He followed Joseph Campbell's mythic journey[28] and embraced his calling. He internalized the Jedi way and worked to pass on what he learned. And in the sequels, after it fell apart, he stepped forward to serve as a beacon of hope once again.

Organized religion offers a place for believers to worship God. Churches are a necessary part of life, bringing worshippers together for a planned interaction with the Holy Trinity and providing the necessary structure for faithful worship. For any of its faults, the Second Vatican Council ushered in a time of great change for the Church in the latter half of the 20th century. The "Novus Ordo (New Order)/Mass of Paul VI"[29] order of masses is accessible, yet beautiful, and is conducted in the vernacular. The congregation is invited to participate fully, as an offering of self.

It is like Christ himself said, "for where two or three are gathered together in my name, there am I in the midst of them, I am there in their midst" (Matthew 18:20). God is then present in all aspects of the mass – the worshippers, the sanctuary, and the Word.

God acts through our priests, who administer the sacraments. Sacraments are seven rituals that give us grace. There are three types in Catholic dogma — Initiation, Vocation, and Healing. The Sacraments of Vocation can only be given once in most cases and are Holy Matrimony (or being single, in a way) and Holy Orders (becoming a clergy member). The Sacraments of Healing can be taken as often as possible consist of Reconciliation/Penance and Anointing of the Sick. The next group is the Sacraments of Initiation, which can be given only once — Baptism, which erases original sin, and Confirmation, which brings young Catholics officially into the church.

The last sacrament is an interesting case. Catholics are obligated to receive transubstantiated Eucharist at least once a week at mass. The first time is extremely special and can only be celebrated once as an act of Initiation, our First Communion. The reason is, Catholics are expected to have a mature understanding of the body and blood before receiving the sacrament.

The Catholic Church is led by the Pope, Jesus' earthly representative and the "servant of the people". He resides in Vatican City, the world's smallest sovereignty. The Vatican has long been the seat of the Catholic faith, and it is full of priceless artifacts. The Vatican was sacked during the 30 Years War, but the city, and our faith, survived.

No other faith has a leader analogous to the pope, yet the tradition dated back to the founding of the church. The first pope was St. Peter, the apostle who denied Jesus three times, yet was given the keys to the kingdom. The Holy Spirit came to him and a vision and gave him the keys to heaven. Peter did much for the early faith, leading the apostles in countless acts of mercy, until he was executed.

Erasmus, in his work The Praise of Folly[30] stated God has a sense of humor. Actually, his exact words, when quoting the apostle Paul, are "The Foolishness of God is wiser than men."[5-2] God is automatically the founder of human humor as He is the creator of all the Earth. Sometimes I think other religions, such as exist as a divine joke; something to occupy humans and teach them to play nice. That is not to disparage them; sincerely held beliefs are a virtue and proper aspiration for a good life.

Or maybe it's not a joke. Maybe God deliberately sent angels to inspire other spiritual leaders like the Dalai Lama and Mohammed. This gives the inhabitants of Earth several choices when it comes to religion. Of course, some 'religions,' like Wicca, which worship nature, are just wrong. Those religions see nature as divine because it is something they do not understand.

The Constitution of the US defines the separation of church and state – that is, the government shall not prohibit the free expression thereof. This is good; a theocracy is not a democracy. The Church cannot run the government; religious solutions to every problem would be disastrous. Neither can the government control religious issues. There are some things that cannot wait for prayer. I would argue, however, there is no real separation if the government is based on morality.

On that note, I profess my love for democracy. I have as much power to sway your mind as does a multi-millionaire lobbyist in Washington. It is an empowering feeling.

CHAPTER 10

Space-Time Continuum

"Crazy thing is... it's true. The Force, the Jedi. All of it. It's all true."[31]

Fun fact, according to the lore, the blur of hyperspace is the elongated view of stars that the ships are passing by. The hyperdrive engines are powered by "hyper matter", with coaxium serving as a sort of nitro boost. Holograms allow for cross-galaxy communications. And bacta is a miraculous healing substance. The technology of the galaxy far, far away is beyond that of our own, even after living under the power of the Sith for a generation.

"Help me, Stephen Hawking. You are my only hope,"[32] to turn a phrase. The man spends his time looking out at the infinite universe, trying to trump Einstein by finding the answer to everything (may he rest in peace). I have dedicated my life to finding something similar, the answer to happiness, bringing meaning to our insignificant life on a small planet among trillions.

The Big Bang Theory was originally proposed by Georges Lemaître, a scientist and Roman Catholic Priest.[33] The theory states approximately 15 billion (yes, billion with a B) years ago the universe started as a mere subatomic particle, astronomically hot and pressurized. It exploded with incalculable force (The Bang) and the universe was born. The Holy Trinity, present before, during, and after initiated the process.

I may have lost skeptics at this point. How could anything be present in the great nothingness before the universe? The simple answer is the Holy Trinity transcends all boundaries. He is an omnipotent being, able to see everywhere at once and touch everyone. He has no physical form; humans are said to be made in 'His image,' in a manner said to be close to perfection. He is described as being forever and has always been. He is also perfect in every way and is dedicated to spreading peace and goodness in this world. He loves us and is our protector. A plane as it relates to mathematics is a surface, infinitesimally small and extending infinitely in every direction. As beings living in four dimensions, our lives are attached to a single plane, whereas someone (or something) extending into more dimensions can do things impossible for us. A metaphor could be a circle (infinite area on a closed surface) to our one plane.

Perhaps the Holy Trinity is a remnant from another universe; perhaps the universe is a cycle, dying and renewing every few trillion years. Because God is so mysterious and beyond our comprehension, we may never know. Anyway, back to the history of the universe.

Over time, the gases and dust cooled. They developed gravitational attractions to each other. According to Albert Einstein, gravity is not an attractive force as Isaac Newton theorized.[34] Instead, large heavy objects (such as a planet) create 'bends' in space, and objects fall into these bends, therefore orbiting. As objects orbited, they gathered speed and mass, eventually coalescing into stars. In their intense cores nuclear fission resulted in the creation of heavier atoms than hydrogen. These were expelled and coalesced into other objects, including our humble planet. Clusters of stars grouped together into galaxies, both large and small. Scientists believe most galaxies have a black hole at their center. Such a coincidence can only be a result of the laws God put into place.

As this was happening, the universe was expanding. Everything in our reality takes place in the universe; the universe is infinite. Yet it is still expanding. How it can be infinite and expanding is a great cosmological mystery. We do not know what is outside the borders. Another universe or maybe an anti-universe? Humans are far from understanding. The universe has been proven to be expanding by the red shift—as objects move away, they emit light on the red side of the visual spectrum (ROYGBIV). Another interesting property of light is how fast it moves—a paltry 300,000 kilometers per second. It is impossible for an object to travel at this speed due to a time dilation effect (also theorized by Einstein). Basically, the faster an object goes, the slower time goes. Someone traveling at such speeds will age slower than someone on Earth. This can be used for a one-way trip to the future. Time travel to the past is mathematically impossible for a variety of reasons with temporal distortions and whatnot, as are wormholes. Future research, however, might prove this wrong.

I could fill an entire book theorizing about time travel. From a simple perspective, changing even a small event could have untold consequences. Pebble in the water, as the metaphor goes.

Another thing belonging in this chapter is the paranormal—magic and ghosts. Did you know there is a difference between 'magic' and "magik?" The former refers to stage tricks, the latter to the manipulation of forces. I have become certain that the paranormal/supernatural really exists. It seems to be unlikely, but there is evidence for it. If it does, it would have to be monitored by God, who is beyond our knowledge. Actually, there is a difference between Catholic and catholic. The capital letter refers to the faith group; the lower letter means universal, as I mentioned in a previous chapter.

Faith and Star battles

The pursuit of the paranormal can be dangerous; these forces are beyond our understanding. One has the potential to go astray, even with the best intentions.

We all know the superstitions about black cats and Friday the 13th. Like many things in our lives, these are steeped in reality. Black cats were associated with witches because the old spinsters of villages kept them. All the churches cracked down on anything which might affect their power, and eliminated women and men who were different, branding them as witches. They were hunted down, given mock trials and executed.

The superstition about Friday the 13th came from October 13, 1307, when the members of the Knights Templar, a Christian order, were simultaneously arrested under orders by Pope Clement V.[35] The superstition which led to throwing salt over our shoulders came from the Greeks in order to thwart bad spirits.

For Crop Circles, I wonder: extraterrestrial messages or home-grown prank? Evidence goes either way. The question is, if they are real, why? Are aliens watching us, judging, and waiting until we are ready? Or is it a space joke? Surely humans don't have the premium on folly.

CHAPTER 11

Origin of the Earth

"Permission to jump in an X-wing and blow something up?"[36]

Again, according to the lore, the Star Wars® galaxy was created much the same way that ours was. Young Anakin Skywalker possessed a desire to see every planet, having a dream of exploration and escaping his slavery (which the Jedi help with). His spirit, although eventually was drawn into the dark side, is certainly something to emulate. Lucas' first released film also dealt with the theme of breaking away from the ties that bind (and as an homage to the number in that film's title appears many times in the saga).

I do not believe the Earth was created in seven days; instead it took millions of years, explained in the preceding chapter. The real issue is the origin of life. Both the Bible and Darwin were wrong, because both cannot be proven using existing evidence. I believe the world formed, and God raised his hand to spring forth the DNA for plants, animals, and sea life.

If God is perfect, why would He neglect to give Adam a mate? That is one of the reasons believe that the Book of Genesis is merely metaphorical. The Book serves as a metaphor for the real creation.

At the same time, it is folly to think humans evolved from monkeys in Africa.

There is also the ever-popular theory saying aliens seeded life on the Earth. Speaking of aliens, we are not alone. It is folly to think the Holy Trinity created life only on one planet. They would most likely been created at the same time. Did Jesus have to go and die for them, too? Probably.

Humans share 50% of our DNA with bananas. This either means we have a common evolutionary ancestor, or God just wants life to be similar and yet diverse, a quite logical idea.

It has happened. Scientists have proven the universe will end in ice. It looks as if Robert Frost is right. As the universe expands, the myriad galaxies will drift further and further apart. As this happens, their energy will entropy and everything will quietly die. That is, if God chooses not to end time before this. The end of time could come at any time; it is His prerogative. Indeed, we are told in the Bible we do not know the time of His arrival and are to be prepared. The end of time will be Jesus' second coming, prophesized all the way back to his death on a cross. Catholics do not believe in the Rapture, or a battle between good and evil where the faithful are ascended and the rest are left on purgatory on Earth. No, just a simple ending. The dead will be resurrected, as the Nicene Creed states. That is, restored fully to body and soul at the end of time in a fulfillment. Although, this refers to those in hell, since after death our souls continue. The just and unjust will be separated. Will there be lights? I think Jesus will descend from heaven; a scene larger than life.
The Left Behind Series offers a powerful witness for the Rapture, but it is nothing more than Christian fantasy.[37] God loves us too much to take our loved ones and leave us in tribulations. The movie version is slightly disturbing. There is no Anti-Christ! We are

responsible for saving our world. Or more specifically, the concept of anti-Christ is simply one who rejects Jesus.

The last book in the Bible, Revelation, is similar to Genesis because it speaks to us in metaphors. The book offers many viewpoints as to how the world will end, including the actions of the 'Four horsemen of the Apocalypse,' Conquest, Death, War, Plague. People take this as symbolism and look for signs. It is impossible to predict the date, even though some said it was 12-21-12. Again, hogwash. It could be tomorrow, 10,000 years, or the death of the sun. Of course, that brings up an interesting point. If the earth is gone, humans could still exist out in the universe. Will God collect their souls as well? Purely theoretical right now, but worth a thought. I'm not going to go as far as saying that human survival will be out in the stars, but it is worth trying.

CHAPTER 12

Prayer

"Some things are stronger than blood. Confronting fear is the destiny of a Jedi...your destiny."[38]

The Living Force may set destinies, but the Jedi can let it speak to them when meditating. Opening them up allows them to even see the will of the Force or see a vision. That allows them to see places, the future/past, or old friends long gone. Such meditation is rarely seen in the saga, but it is an essential part of a Jedi's life. They are able to connect to the Force through the midichlorians, which are symbiotic lifeforms living in their blood. When George Lucas went to produce the prequel trilogy, he added this concept to deepen the understanding of the Force.

I am not sure if I can give this chapter the respect it deserves, but here goes. Prayer is a beautiful act, where you interact with God, or "communion with Christ." Prayer can take place in a variety of ways. You and God can have a dialogue, though God is best at listening. Even if you rant, God is there for us. It does not matter if you pray something from the bottom of your heart or pray one of the official church prayers. Each night, I pray three different ways, to each part of the Holy Trinity. My thanks go to God, and I offer supplications up to Jesus. Any special intentions go to the Holy Spirit.

The reasons for prayer vary as much as our species. The most common reason is to ask for help. The "proper form" of prayer is that it should arise from the heart. Perhaps you had a bad day, or you are having trouble paying the rent. Another reason might be you are having spiritual issues. Several people have said "God helps those who help themselves." Although it's a little on the selfish side to ask for material goods from God, asking for help on many other matters is encouraged. No matter what, God is there for us, because is love is stronger than the gravity from a black hole. Prayer gives us a feeling of peace. In many Christian denominations it is customary to say 'amen' at the end of each prayer. It is a Hebrew word closely meaning "so be it." Not to be confused with "so say we all."[39]

The main types of prayers are supplication, praise, intercessory, and thanksgiving. These are fairly self-explanatory; to offer praise is to bring forward words of adoration for God's good works and deeds. A prayer of supplication is to request something. Intercessory prayers are requests on behalf of another. And thanksgiving is simply to raise up words of thanks. These messages are a powerful tool for building our faith life and supporting our relationships. I also was recently introduced to the spirituality of Saint Ignatius. His Daily Examen is a powerful meditation and prayer.

Like I said above, I like to mix up these types in my daily routine.

Catholics have a special prayer known as The Rosary, and we use a string of beads to keep count. The beads developed from the 150 ones used by monks to chant the Psalms. Nowadays, we say less than 150 prayers. We start with the apostle's Creed, then three Hail Maries asking for an increase in faith, hope, and love. Afterwards, we start the five decades. Each decade consists of one of the Mysteries, ten Hail Maries, and an Our Father. There are four types of mysteries — Sorrowful (Jesus' death), Joyful (Jesus' birth),

Luminous (the start of Jesus' ministry) and the Glorious Mystery (miracles after Jesus' death). The Rosary Bead itself is a religious object, or sacramental. We use it to talk in a special way to Mary. We can also meditate during the prayer over the Mysteries.

During the long hiatus mentioned in chapter one, I struggled a lot over prayer. There was a lot of raging, to be honest. But God answered the deepest longings of my heart. He sent an "angel" my way, leading to a restoration and strengthening of my faith. It awakened a new desire for a fuller prayer life and a restored appreciation for the beauty and ritual of the mass.

The question is, does God answer our prayers? Absolutely, stupendously, yes, I say. Maybe not in the way we exactly desire or even figure, but in a better way for ourselves. Especially if what we are asking is dangerous. He hears all our prayers, whether we are crying for help or interceding for another.

CHAPTER 13

Paradise

"Truly wonderful, the mind of a child is."[40]

There was a debate in fandom in the mid-oughts about Jedi hubris and how they were rightfully struck down in Order 66. I don't ascribe to that. Sure, they were indeed blinded by their own arrogance and the shroud of the dark side, but their strength and compassion are aspirational. As the Jedi Council says, they are peacekeepers.[4-1]

I feel as though more needs to be discussed about paradise, both the earthly and spiritual versions. As I mentioned above, heaven lies outside our plane of existence. It is a place where souls of humans go after death. Heaven is a place to worship God for all eternity. The Bible has direct explanations of this fact. Sorry. It is not a place where you can golf all day or eat doughnuts. Indeed, it is a place of love for the fully idealized self. "Luminous beings are we"[3-1] as the quote goes.

Faith and Star battles

Many question the nature of heaven. They say things about how only "true believers" can enter in. Again, this is not the case. Heaven is open to ALL if they live a life of morality and believe in higher powers. Angels--heavenly spirits live in heaven and offer eternal praise to God. The official, catechumenal answer is that heaven is indeed not a place; rather it is everywhere. It is a state of mind.

The earthly version was depicted as a parable in the Book of Genesis. It was where Adam and Eve lived after creation along with all the animals, and a special tree. The tree was the Tree of Knowledge, and the two were forbidden to eat its fruit. Adam was tasked with naming the animals, and was perfect as possible without being God, and was also immortal. Every other beast was paired with a mate, except Adam. God put him in a trance and took out a rib. He formed Eve, known as woman—from man. They lived in happiness, except for one thing. The serpent came to Eve and tricked her into eating the apple, who in turn gave it to Adam.

The two gained knowledge and came to realize they were not wearing clothes. Afraid, they hid from God, who subsequently found them and admonished them for their betrayal. He threw them out of the garden and guarded the entrance with a flaming sword and an angel.

Afterward, they were destined to die and live with suffering. Their first two sons, Cain and Abel showed what results from human arrogance. Cain became jealous of Abel and murdered him.

God put a mark on Cain. He then told Adam and Eve to go forth and multiply, and they seeded the world. Interesting story—the character of Kane in Command & Conquer is hinted to be Cain himself (since revealed to be an alien).[41]

Even if we did not come after Adam and Eve, for some reasons humans are trying their best to go back to a state of perfection, which is impossible until the time of the Kingdom of God comes. This quest for perfection is what drives humanity's search for a better life, including immortality. That leads to an interesting line of thought. If Adam was brought wholesale into existence, how did language develop?

Another reason humans search for meaning in life is suffering. Christians believe human suffering came from Adam and Eve (original sin). There can be redemption in suffering, even from the darkest badness, good can be found. No bones about it, that is not an easy concept for us to accept at times. But for others, redemptive suffering is actually comforting.

Catholics also have the concept of Purgatory, which is a spot for purification and erasing the stain of sin prior to entering heaven. There are scriptural references for the purification or "have washed their robes and made them white in the blood of the Lamb" (Chapter 7 in Revelation) to create purity of the soul for heaven.

We are heading towards a single ecumenical culture. Instant communication breaks down borders. Economies affect each other the world over. Good or bad? I don't know. Although I certainly like to believe that globalism is a positive force. May God bless us as we move forward.

And remember, the Force will be with you, always.

CHAPTER 14

Review

"What our mothers and father fought for; we will not let die. Not today. Today we make our last stand, for the galaxy. For Leia. For everyone we've lost."[42]

I thought it would be helpful to include a review of my major points.

I wrote this to logically bring awareness to issues.
Who am I? Thomas Myers, autistic guy and procrastinating creative.
Christian Dogma says there is One God, but three persons--The Father, Son, and Spirit.
God Is – the logos itself.
Mary was a virgin when she bore Jesus.
Sex is an expression of love.
Human nature is beastly, but society makes us good.
Humans are created equal.
The Bible is the ultimate resource about God.
Some aspects of the supernatural exist.
Science opens up our awareness about the physical universe, but

some lines should never be crossed.
All things in our lives happen for a reason.
Organized religion is necessary.
God lies outside our plane of existence.
The universe is expanding.
Neither Darwin nor Genesis was correct.
We cannot know the hour of Jesus' return.
Prayer is a wonderful way to communicate with God.
Paradise is heaven; our souls are with God and offer him eternal praise.
The Garden of Eden does not exist.
What is progress?
George Lucas is a visionary.
    I am a nerd. See if you can find all the subtle references.
Have hope.

References

Brilliant Minds: Secrets of the Cosmos. Discovery Channel, 2003. 10-3

The Hero with a Thousand Faces. Campbell, Joseph. Pantheon Books, 1949. 9-1

Catechism of the Catholic Church (2nd ed.). (1997). 2-4

Cheung, Tommy. "Jediism: Religion at Law?" *Oxford Journal of Law and Religion,* Volume 8, Issue 2, June 2019.8-2

"Command & Conquer." Westwood Studios, 1995.13-1

"Command & Conquer: Tiberian Sun." Westwood Studios, 1999.

Erasmus, Desiderius. *The Praise of Folly*, 1509.

"Forced Abortions." http://www.onenewsnow.com/Culture/Default.aspx?id=3 78732. 1/11/2001. 1-3

Frost, Robert. "Fire and Ice," 1916.

"Home Soil." Star Trek: The Next Generation. Broadcast 02-22-88.7-2

"History Stories: Why Friday the 13th Spelled Doom for the Knights Templar." https://www.history.com/news/why-friday-the-13th-spelled-doom-for-the-knights-templar 10-4

"I am Legend." Dir: Francis Lawrence. Perf: Will Smith, Alice Braga. Warner Brothers, 2007.

Jefferson, Thomas. "The Declaration of Independence." Philadelphia, 1776.

John, Paul II. *Encyclical Letter Evangelium Vitae*. Washington, D.C: United States Catholic Conference, 1995. Print.

Kant, Immanuel. *The Metaphysical Elements of Justice: Part I of the Metaphysics of Morals*. 1797.4-2

LaHaye, Tim and Jerry Jenkins. *Left Behind*, Tyndale House Publishers, 1995. 11-2

Lewis, C.S. *The Screwtape Letters*. 1942. 2-7

Locke, John. *Essay Concerning Human Understanding*. 1689.5-3

Milton, John. *Paradise Lost*. 1667.

"Mobile Suit Gundam Wing." Bandai, 1995.

Pernoud, Régine; Clin, Marie-Véronique. *Joan of Arc*. St. Martin's Press, (1998).2-5

"Pro-Life Day Of Silent Solidarity." http://silentday.org/. Updated Daily. Accessed October 2008. 1-2

Wes Farrell and Bert Berns. Hang on Sloopy. Hang on Sloopy. 1965. Single. Bang. Video. 3-2

"Robotech: The Macross Saga." Harmony Gold, 1985.

Saint Augustine. Augustine on the nature of the Sacrament of the Eucharist" Sermon 272. 2-6

Shelley, Mary. *Frankenstein*, 1818.

"Spiderman." Dir: Sam Raimi. Perf: Toby MacGuire, Kirsten Dunst, Willem Dafoe. Columbia Pictures, 2002.7-1

Spirit, Holy et al. *The Holy Bible*, King James Version, Cambridge University Press, 1611, original version circa 8000 BC, second edition 397 AD.

Soter, Steven; Tyson, Neil Degrasse. *Cosmic Horizons: Astronomy at the Cutting Edge*. New Press, 2000.10-2

"Star Wars: Episode I The Phantom Menace" Dir: George Lucas. Perf: Liam Neeson, Ewan McGregor, Natalie Portman, Jake Lloyd, Pernilla August, Frank Oz, Ian McDiarmid, Oliver Ford Davis, Hugh Quarshie, Ahmed Best Anthony Daniels, Kenny Baker. Lucasfilm LTD., 1999.

"Star Wars: Episode II Attack of the Clones" Dir: George Lucas. Ewan McGregor, Natalie Portman, Hayden Christensen, Frank Oz, Pernilla August, Temeura Morrison, Ian McDiarmid, Oliver Ford Davis, Ahmed Best Anthony Daniels, Kenny Baker, Silas Carson, Samuel Jackson, Christopher Lee. Lucasfilm LTD., 2002.

"Star Wars: Episode III Revenge of the Sith" Dir: George Lucas. Perf: Ewan McGregor, Natalie Portman, Hayden Christensen, Frank Oz, Jimmy Smits, Peter Mayhew, Ian McDiarmid, Oliver Ford Davis, Temeura Morrison, Ahmed Best Anthony Daniels, Kenny Baker, Silas Carson, Samuel Jackson, Christopher Lee. Lucasfilm LTD., 2005.

"Star Wars: Episode IV A New Hope" Dir: George Lucas. Perf: Mark Hamil, Carrie Fisher, Harrison Ford, Anthony Daniels, Kenny Baker, Alec Guinness, Peter Cushing, Peter Mayhew, David Prowse, Jack Purvise, Eddie Byrne. Lucasfilm LTD., 1977.

"Star Wars: Episode V The Empire Strikes Back" Dir: Irving Kershner. Perf: Mark Hamil, Peter Mayhew, Carrie Fisher, Harrison Ford, Anthony Daniels, Peter Mayhew, David Prowse, Kenny Baker, Frank Oz, Billy Dee Williams. Lucasfilm LTD., 1980.

"Star Wars: Episode VI Return of the Jedi" Dir: Richard Marquand. Perf: Mark Hamil, Carrie Fisher, Peter Mayhew, Harrison Ford, Anthony Daniels, Peter Mayhew, Sebastian Shaw, Ian McDiarmid, James Earl Jones, Frank Oz, David Prowse, Billy Dee Williams, Alec Guinness. Lucasfilm LTD., 1983.

"Star Wars: Episode VII The Force Awakens" Dir: J. J. Abrams. Perf: Mark Hamil, Carrie Fisher, Harrison Ford, Peter Mayhew, Anthony Daniels, Daisy Ridley, Oscar Isaac, John Boyega, Adam Driver, Lupita Nyong'o, Andy Serkis, Domhnall Gleeson, Max Von Sydow, Gwendoline Christie, Ken Leung, Greg Grunberg, . Lucasfilm LTD., 2015.

"Star Wars: Episode VII The Last Jedi" Dir: Rian Johnson. Perf: Mark Hamil, Carrie Fisher, Harrison Ford, Anthony Daniels, Joonas Suotamo, Daisy Ridley, Oscar Isaac, John Boyega, Adam Driver, Lupita Nyong'o, Andy Serkis, Domhnall Gleeson, Gwendoline Christie, Kelly Marie Tran, Laura Dern, Frank Oz, Benicio Del Toro. Lucasfilm LTD., 2017.

"Star Wars: Episode IX The Rise of Skywalker" Dir: J. J. Abrams. Perf: Mark Hamil, Carrie Fisher, Harrison Ford, Anthony Daniels, Joonas Suotamo, Daisy Ridley, Oscar Isaac, John Boyega, Adam Driver, Lupita Nyong'o, Ian McDiarmid, Domhnall Gleeson, Billy Dee Williams, Kelly Marie Tran, Keri Russel, Richard Grant, Naomie Ackie, Greg Grunberg, Shirley Henderson, Billie Lourde, Dominic Monaghan. Lucasfilm LTD., 2019.

"Star Wars: The Force Unleashed." LucasArts, 2008. State Of Ohio Private/Public Education Curriculums at St. Cecilia Elementary School and Central Crossing High School.

"The Scandal of the Incarnation." Celebration. December 2006, 35:12.

USCCB. "Understanding the Bible." http://www.usccb.org/bible/understanding-the-bible/index.cfm. Accessed January 12, 2020.6-1
Wales, Jimmy. "Wikipedia." Wikipedia.org. Created 2001. Accessed December 21, 2012.

https://www.usccb.org/prayer-and-worship/prayers-and-devotions/rosaries/how-to-pray-the-rosary

Endnotes

1 *Star Wars Episode VI: Return of the Jedi* (Twentieth Century Fox Home Entertainment, 1983).
2 " 'Pro-Life Day Of Silent Solidarity.' ," Day of Silence, accessed 2008, http://silentday.org/.
3 *Star Wars Episode IX: The Rise of Skywalker* (Disney, 2019).
4 *Star Wars Episode VI: Return of the Jedi* (Twentieth Century Fox Home Entertainment, 1983).
5 Rich Heffern, "The Scandal of the Incarnation.,'" *Celebration*, no. 35 (2006).
6 *Catechism of the Catholic Church.* (1992).
7 Pernoud Régine, Marie-Veronique Clin, and Jeremy DuQuesnay Adams, *Joan of Arc: Her Story* (London: Phoenix, 2000).
8 Saint Augustine, *Sermon 272*, ed. John Rotelle, trans. Edmund Hill, 3rd ed., vol. 7 (Hyde Park, NY: Rotelle series, 1993).
9 Saint Augustine, *Sermon 272*, ed. John Rotelle, trans. Edmund Hill, 3rd ed., vol. 7 (Hyde Park, NY: Rotelle series, 1993).
10 C. S. Lewis, *The Screwtape Letters* (Geoffrey Bles, 1942).
11 "Bishop Fulton J. Sheen: Life Is Worth Living." n.d. Fulton J. Sheen Company, Inc. Accessed January 14, 2021. https://www.bishopsheen.com/.
12 *Star Wars Episode V: The Empire Strikes Back* (Twentieth Century Fox Home Entertainment, 1980).
13 The McCoys. "Hang on Sloopy." *Hang On Sloopy*.
14 Norris, Charles W. 2012. "Pope John Paul II, Humanae Vitae, and the Theology of the Body - Homiletic & Pastoral Review." Homiletic & Pastoral Review. February 3, 2012. https://www.hprweb.com/2012/02/pope-john-paul-ii-humanae-vitae-and-the-theology-of-the-body/.
15 *Star Wars Episode II: Attack of the Clones* (Twentieth Century

Fox Home Entertainment, 2002).
[16] *Star Wars Episode IV: A New Hope* (Twentieth Century Fox Home Entertainment, 1983).
[17] "Conservation of Energy," NASA (NASA), accessed October 28, 2020, https://www.grc.nasa.gov/WWW/K-12/airplane/thermo1f.html.
[18] *Star Wars Episode I: The Phantom Menace* (Twentieth Century Fox Home Entertainment, 1983).
[19] *Star Wars Episode IV: A New Hope* (Twentieth Century Fox Home Entertainment, 1983).
[20] John Locke, *An Essay Concerning Human Understanding. In Four Books. Written by John Locke, Gent* (Dublin: Printed by and for W. Sleater, H. Chamberlaine, and J. Potts, 1786).
[21] *Star Wars Episode V: The Empire Strikes Back* (Twentieth Century Fox Home Entertainment, 1980).
[22] *Star Wars Episode IV: A New Hope* (Twentieth Century Fox Home Entertainment, 1977).
[23] *Spider-Man* (Columbia TriStar Home Entertainment, 2002).
[24] "Home Soil." *Star Trek: The Next Generation* (Paramount, 22 Feb. 1988).
[25] *Star Wars Episode III: Revenge of the Sith* (Twentieth Century Fox Home Entertainment, 2005).
[26] Tommy Cheung, "Jediism: Religion at Law?," *Oxford Journal of Law and Religion* 8, no. 2 (June 2019): pp. 350-377, https://doi.org/10.1093/ojlr/rwz010.
[27] *Star Wars Episode IV: A New Hope* (Twentieth Century Fox Home Entertainment, 1977).
[28] Campbell, *The Hero with a Thousand Faces* (New York: Pantheon Books, 1968).
[29] M. A., Political Theory, and Political Theory B. A. n.d. "What Is the Novus Ordo in the Catholic Church?" Learn Religions. Accessed January 14, 2021. https://www.learnreligions.com/what-is-the-novus-ordo-542952.
[30] Desiderius Erasmus and Hans Holbein, *The Praise of Folly* (London: Hamilton, Adams, 1887).
[31] *Star Wars Episode VII: The Force Awakens* (Disney, 2015).

32 Steven Soter, *Cosmic Horizons: Astronomy at the Cutting Edge* (New York, NY: New Press, 2001).

33 Sack, Harald. 2019. "Georges Lemaître and the Origins of the Big Bang Theory." SciHi Blog. June 20, 2019. http://scihi.org/george-lemaitre-big-bang-theory/.

34 "Einstein's Theory and Gravity | American Museum of Natural History." 2021. American Museum of Natural History. 2021. https://www.amnh.org/exhibitions/einstein/gravity.

35 Barbara Maranzani, "Why Friday the 13th Spelled Doom for the Knights Templar," History.com (A&E Television Networks, October 13, 2017), https://www.history.com/news/why-friday-the-13th-spelled-doom-for-the-knights-templar.

36 *Star Wars Episode VIII: The Last Jedi* (Disney, 2017).

37 LaHaye, Tim and Jerry Jenkins. *Left Behind* (Tyndale House Publishers, 1995.)

38 *Star Wars Episode IX: T9he Rise of Skywalker* (Disney, 2019).

39 Posted by Rabbi Harvey, "'Amen and Amen,'" Rabbi Mike Harvey, September 23, 2016, https://rabbiharvey.wordpress.com/2016/09/23/amen-and-amen/.

40 *Star Wars Episode II: Attack of the Clones* (Twentieth Century Fox Home Entertainment, 2002).

41 *Command & Conquer* (Westwood Studios, 1995).

42 *Star Wars Episode IX: The Rise of Skywalker* (Disney, 2019).

About the Author

The thirty-year-old author was born in raised in Columbus, OH. He attended Central Crossing High School in Grove City. He currently attends an online program through Arizona State University. He was previously at The Ohio State University, where he was extremely busy in a Political Science Major, the Politics, Society, and Law Scholars Program, and a job with Campus Dining Services. His interests include pop-culture franchises and inspiring others. He wants you to know how much of a nerd he is, and how much of an impact his family has on his life. Thomas also wants to thank all those who made his life so amazing!

This is his first published work, if it does get published.

Visit me at https://thomasmusings.com

"God bless you all, and never tell me the odds."

www.ingramcontent.com/pod-product-compliance
Lightning Source LLC
Chambersburg PA
CBHW050334120526
44592CB00014B/2175